THE Art OF THE CAT

January 2025 - June 2026

18 MONTH WEEKLY PLANNER & ORGANIZER

Nola Lee Kelsey

Soggy Nomad Press
Las Vegas, NV, USA

ISBN: 978-1-957532-54-7

Cover design by Nola Lee Kelsey

2025

January

S	M	T	W	T	F	S
			1	2	3	4
5	6	7	8	9	10	11
12	13	14	15	16	17	18
19	20	21	22	23	24	25
26	27	28	29	30	31	

February

S	M	T	W	T	F	S
						1
2	3	4	5	6	7	8
9	10	11	12	13	14	15
16	17	18	19	20	21	22
23	24	25	26	27	28	

March

S	M	T	W	T	F	S
						1
2	3	4	5	6	7	8
9	10	11	12	13	14	15
16	17	18	19	20	21	22
23	24	25	26	27	28	29
30	31					

April

S	M	T	W	T	F	S
		1	2	3	4	5
6	7	8	9	10	11	12
13	14	15	16	17	18	19
20	21	22	23	24	25	26
27	28	29	30			

May

S	M	T	W	T	F	S
				1	2	3
4	5	6	7	8	9	10
11	12	13	14	15	16	17
18	19	20	21	22	23	24
25	26	27	28	29	30	31

June

S	M	T	W	T	F	S
1	2	3	4	5	6	7
8	9	10	11	12	13	14
15	16	17	18	19	20	21
22	23	24	25	26	27	28
29	30					

July

S	M	T	W	T	F	S
		1	2	3	4	5
6	7	8	9	10	11	12
13	14	15	16	17	18	19
20	21	22	23	24	25	26
27	28	29	30	31		

August

S	M	T	W	T	F	S
					1	2
3	4	5	6	7	8	9
10	11	12	13	14	15	16
17	18	19	20	21	22	23
24	25	26	27	28	29	30
31						

September

S	M	T	W	T	F	S
	1	2	3	4	5	6
7	8	9	10	11	12	13
14	15	16	17	18	19	20
21	22	23	24	25	26	27
28	29	30				

October

S	M	T	W	T	F	S
			1	2	3	4
5	6	7	8	9	10	11
12	13	14	15	16	17	18
19	20	21	22	23	24	25
26	27	28	29	30	31	

November

S	M	T	W	T	F	S
						1
2	3	4	5	6	7	8
9	10	11	12	13	14	15
16	17	18	19	20	21	22
23	24	25	26	27	28	29
30						

December

S	M	T	W	T	F	S
	1	2	3	4	5	6
7	8	9	10	11	12	13
14	15	16	17	18	19	20
21	22	23	24	25	26	27
28	29	30	31			

2026

January

S	M	T	W	T	F	S
				1	2	3
4	5	6	7	8	9	10
11	12	13	14	15	16	17
18	19	20	21	22	23	24
25	26	27	28	29	30	31

February

S	M	T	W	T	F	S
1	2	3	4	5	6	7
8	9	10	11	12	13	14
15	16	17	18	19	20	21
22	23	24	25	26	27	28

March

S	M	T	W	T	F	S
1	2	3	4	5	6	7
8	9	10	11	12	13	14
15	16	17	18	19	20	21
22	23	24	25	26	27	28
29	30	31				

April

S	M	T	W	T	F	S
			1	2	3	4
5	6	7	8	9	10	11
12	13	14	15	16	17	18
19	20	21	22	23	24	25
26	27	28	29	30		

May

S	M	T	W	T	F	S
					1	2
3	4	5	6	7	8	9
10	11	12	13	14	15	16
17	18	19	20	21	22	23
24	25	26	27	28	29	30
31						

June

S	M	T	W	T	F	S
	1	2	3	4	5	6
7	8	9	10	11	12	13
14	15	16	17	18	19	20
21	22	23	24	25	26	27
28	29	30				

July

S	M	T	W	T	F	S
			1	2	3	4
5	6	7	8	9	10	11
12	13	14	15	16	17	18
19	20	21	22	23	24	25
26	27	28	29	30	31	

August

S	M	T	W	T	F	S
						1
2	3	4	5	6	7	8
9	10	11	12	13	14	15
16	17	18	19	20	21	22
23	24	25	26	27	28	29
30	31					

September

S	M	T	W	T	F	S
		1	2	3	4	5
6	7	8	9	10	11	12
13	14	15	16	17	18	19
20	21	22	23	24	25	26
27	28	29	30			

October

S	M	T	W	T	F	S
				1	2	3
4	5	6	7	8	9	10
11	12	13	14	15	16	17
18	19	20	21	22	23	24
25	26	27	28	29	30	31

November

S	M	T	W	T	F	S
1	2	3	4	5	6	7
8	9	10	11	12	13	14
15	16	17	18	19	20	21
22	23	24	25	26	27	28
29	30					

December

S	M	T	W	T	F	S
		1	2	3	4	5
6	7	8	9	10	11	12
13	14	15	16	17	18	19
20	21	22	23	24	25	26
27	28	29	30	31		

January 2025

Monday 30

Tuesday 31

New Year's Eve

Wednesday 1

New Year's Day

Thursday 2

Friday 3

Saturday 4

Sunday 5

Shopping:

- [ ]
- [ ]
- [ ]
- [ ]
- [ ]
- [ ]
- [ ]
- [ ]
- [ ]
- [ ]
- [ ]
- [ ]

Notes:

January

S	M	T	W	T	F	S
			1	2	3	4
5	6	7	8	9	10	11
12	13	14	15	16	17	18
19	20	21	22	23	24	25
26	27	28	29	30	31	

January 2025

Monday 6

Tuesday 7

Wednesday 8

Thursday 9

Friday 10

Saturday 11

Sunday 12

Shopping:

Notes:

January

S	M	T	W	T	F	S
			1	2	3	4
5	6	7	8	9	10	11
12	13	14	15	16	17	18
19	20	21	22	23	24	25
26	27	28	29	30	31	

January 2025

Monday 13

Tuesday 14

Wednesday 15

Thursday 16

Friday 17

Saturday 18

Sunday 19

Shopping:

- [ ]
- [ ]
- [ ]
- [ ]
- [ ]
- [ ]
- [ ]
- [ ]
- [ ]
- [ ]
- [ ]
- [ ]

Notes:

January

S	M	T	W	T	F	S
			1	2	3	4
5	6	7	8	9	10	11
12	13	14	15	16	17	18
19	20	21	22	23	24	25
26	27	28	29	30	31	

January 2025

Monday 20 Martin Luther King Jr. Day
Tuesday 21
Wednesday 22
Thursday 23
Friday 24
Saturday 25
Sunday 26

Shopping:

- ☐
- ☐
- ☐
- ☐
- ☐
- ☐
- ☐
- ☐
- ☐
- ☐
- ☐
- ☐

Notes:

January

S	M	T	W	T	F	S
			1	2	3	4
5	6	7	8	9	10	11
12	13	14	15	16	17	18
19	20	21	22	23	24	25
26	27	28	29	30	31	

January 2025

Monday 27

Tuesday 28

Wednesday 29

Thursday 30

Friday 31

Saturday 1

Sunday 2

Shopping:

- [ ]
- [ ]
- [ ]
- [ ]
- [ ]
- [ ]
- [ ]
- [ ]
- [ ]
- [ ]
- [ ]
- [ ]

Notes:

January

M	T	W	T	F	S	S
		1	2	3	4	5
6	7	8	9	10	11	12
13	14	15	16	17	18	19
20	21	22	23	24	25	26
27	28	29	30	31		

February 2025

Monday 3

Tuesday 4

Wednesday 5

Thursday 6

Friday 7

Saturday 8

Sunday 9

Shopping:

Notes:

February

M	T	W	T	F	S	S
					1	2
3	4	5	6	7	8	9
10	11	12	13	14	15	16
17	18	19	20	21	22	23
24	25	26	27	28		

February 2025

Monday 10

Tuesday 11

Wednesday 12

Thursday 13

Friday 14

Valentine's Day

Saturday 15

Sunday 16

Shopping:

- [ ]
- [ ]
- [ ]
- [ ]
- [ ]
- [ ]
- [ ]
- [ ]
- [ ]
- [ ]
- [ ]
- [ ]

Notes:

February

M	T	W	T	F	S	S
					1	2
3	4	5	6	7	8	9
10	11	12	13	14	15	16
17	18	19	20	21	22	23
24	25	26	27	28		

February 2025

Monday 17
Washington's Birthday

Tuesday 18

Wednesday 19

Thursday 20

Friday 21

Saturday 22

Sunday 23

Shopping:

Notes:

February

M	T	W	T	F	S	S
					1	2
3	4	5	6	7	8	9
10	11	12	13	14	15	16
17	18	19	20	21	22	23
24	25	26	27	28		

February 2025

Monday 24

Tuesday 25

Wednesday 26

Thursday 27

Friday 28

Saturday 1

Sunday 2

Shopping:

- [ ]
- [ ]
- [ ]
- [ ]
- [ ]
- [ ]
- [ ]
- [ ]
- [ ]
- [ ]
- [ ]
- [ ]

Notes:

February

M	T	W	T	F	S	S
					1	2
3	4	5	6	7	8	9
10	11	12	13	14	15	16
17	18	19	20	21	22	23
24	25	26	27	28		

March 2025

Monday 3

Tuesday 4

Wednesday 5

Thursday 6

Friday 7

Saturday 8

Sunday 9

Shopping:

- [ ]
- [ ]
- [ ]
- [ ]
- [ ]
- [ ]
- [ ]
- [ ]
- [ ]
- [ ]
- [ ]
- [ ]

Notes:

March

M	T	W	T	F	S	S
					1	2
3	4	5	6	7	8	9
10	11	12	13	14	15	16
17	18	19	20	21	22	23
24	25	26	27	28	29	30
31						

March 2025

Monday 10

Tuesday 11

Wednesday 12

Thursday 13

Friday 14

Saturday 15

Sunday 16

Shopping:

- [ ]
- [ ]
- [ ]
- [ ]
- [ ]
- [ ]
- [ ]
- [ ]
- [ ]
- [ ]
- [ ]
- [ ]

Notes:

March

M	T	W	T	F	S	S
					1	2
3	4	5	6	7	8	9
10	11	12	13	14	15	16
17	18	19	20	21	22	23
24	25	26	27	28	29	30
31						

March 2025

Monday 17
St. Patrick's Day

Tuesday 18

Wednesday 19

Thursday 20
Spring has Sprung

Friday 21

Saturday 22

Sunday 23

Shopping:

- [ ]
- [ ]
- [ ]
- [ ]
- [ ]
- [ ]
- [ ]
- [ ]
- [ ]
- [ ]
- [ ]
- [ ]

Notes:

March

M	T	W	T	F	S	S
					1	2
3	4	5	6	7	8	9
10	11	12	13	14	15	16
17	18	19	20	21	22	23
24	25	26	27	28	29	30
31						

March 2025

Monday 24

Tuesday 25

Wednesday 26

Thursday 27

Friday 28

Saturday 29

Sunday 30

Shopping:

Notes:

March

M	T	W	T	F	S	S
					1	2
3	4	5	6	7	8	9
10	11	12	13	14	15	16
17	18	19	20	21	22	23
24	25	26	27	28	29	30
31						

April 2025

Monday 31

Tuesday 1

Wednesday 2

Thursday 3

Friday 4

Saturday 5

Sunday 6

Shopping:

Notes:

April

M	T	W	T	F	S	S
	1	2	3	4	5	6
7	8	9	10	11	12	13
14	15	16	17	18	19	20
21	22	23	24	25	26	27
28	29	30				

April 2025

Monday 7

Tuesday 8

Wednesday 9

Thursday 10

Friday 11

Saturday 12

Sunday 13

Shopping:

Notes:

April

M	T	W	T	F	S	S
	1	2	3	4	5	6
7	8	9	10	11	12	13
14	15	16	17	18	19	20
21	22	23	24	25	26	27
28	29	30				

April 2025

Monday 14

Tuesday 15
Tax Day

Wednesday 16

Thursday 17

Friday 18

Saturday 19

Sunday 20
Easter Sunday

Shopping:

- ☐
- ☐
- ☐
- ☐
- ☐
- ☐
- ☐
- ☐
- ☐
- ☐
- ☐
- ☐

Notes:

April

M	T	W	T	F	S	S
	1	2	3	4	5	6
7	8	9	10	11	12	13
14	15	16	17	18	19	20
21	22	23	24	25	26	27
28	29	30				

April 2025

Monday 21

Tuesday 22

Wednesday 23

Thursday 24

Friday 25

Saturday 26

Sunday 27

Shopping:

- [ ]
- [ ]
- [ ]
- [ ]
- [ ]
- [ ]
- [ ]
- [ ]
- [ ]
- [ ]
- [ ]
- [ ]

Notes:

April

M	T	W	T	F	S	S
	1	2	3	4	5	6
7	8	9	10	11	12	13
14	15	16	17	18	19	20
21	22	23	24	25	26	27
28	29	30				

April 2025

Monday 28

Tuesday 29

Wednesday 30

Thursday 1

Friday 2

Saturday 3

Sunday 4

Shopping:

- [ ]
- [ ]
- [ ]
- [ ]
- [ ]
- [ ]
- [ ]
- [ ]
- [ ]
- [ ]
- [ ]
- [ ]

Notes:

April

M	T	W	T	F	S	S
	1	2	3	4	5	6
7	8	9	10	11	12	13
14	15	16	17	18	19	20
21	22	23	24	25	26	27
28	29	30				

May 2025

Monday 5
Tuesday 6
Wednesday 7
Thursday 8
Friday 9
Saturday 10
Sunday 11 Mother's Day

Shopping:

- [ ]
- [ ]
- [ ]
- [ ]
- [ ]
- [ ]
- [ ]
- [ ]
- [ ]
- [ ]
- [ ]
- [ ]

Notes:

May

M	T	W	T	F	S	S
			1	2	3	4
5	6	7	8	9	10	11
12	13	14	15	16	17	18
19	20	21	22	23	24	25
26	27	28	29	30	31	

May 2025

Monday 12

Tuesday 13

Wednesday 14

Thursday 15

Friday 16

Saturday 17

Sunday 18

Shopping:

Notes:

May

M	T	W	T	F	S	S
			1	2	3	4
5	6	7	8	9	10	11
12	13	14	15	16	17	18
19	20	21	22	23	24	25
26	27	28	29	30	31	

May 2025

Monday 19

Tuesday 20

Wednesday 21

Thursday 22

Friday 23

Saturday 24

Sunday 25

Shopping:

Notes:

May

M	T	W	T	F	S	S
			1	2	3	4
5	6	7	8	9	10	11
12	13	14	15	16	17	18
19	20	21	22	23	24	25
26	27	28	29	30	31	

May 2025

Monday 26
Memorial Day

Tuesday 27

Wednesday 28

Thursday 29

Friday 30

Saturday 31

Sunday 1

Shopping:

- [ ]
- [ ]
- [ ]
- [ ]
- [ ]
- [ ]
- [ ]
- [ ]
- [ ]
- [ ]
- [ ]
- [ ]

Notes:

May

M	T	W	T	F	S	S
			1	2	3	4
5	6	7	8	9	10	11
12	13	14	15	16	17	18
19	20	21	22	23	24	25
26	27	28	29	30	31	

June 2025

Monday 2

Tuesday 3

Wednesday 4

Thursday 5

Friday 6

Saturday 7

Sunday 8

Shopping:

- [ ]
- [ ]
- [ ]
- [ ]
- [ ]
- [ ]
- [ ]
- [ ]
- [ ]
- [ ]
- [ ]
- [ ]

Notes:

June

M	T	W	T	F	S	S
						1
2	3	4	5	6	7	8
9	10	11	12	13	14	15
16	17	18	19	20	21	22
23	24	25	26	27	28	29
30						

June 2025

Monday 9

Tuesday 10

Wednesday 11

Thursday 12

Friday 13

Saturday 14

Sunday 15

Father's Day

Shopping:

Notes:

June

M	T	W	T	F	S	S
						1
2	3	4	5	6	7	8
9	10	11	12	13	14	15
16	17	18	19	20	21	22
23	24	25	26	27	28	29
30						

June 2025

Monday 16

Tuesday 17

Wednesday 18

Thursday 19

Juneteenth

Friday 20

It's Summer!

Saturday 21

Sunday 22

Shopping:

- [ ]
- [ ]
- [ ]
- [ ]
- [ ]
- [ ]
- [ ]
- [ ]
- [ ]
- [ ]
- [ ]
- [ ]

Notes:

June

M	T	W	T	F	S	S
						1
2	3	4	5	6	7	8
9	10	11	12	13	14	15
16	17	18	19	20	21	22
23	24	25	26	27	28	29
30						

June 2025

Monday 23

Tuesday 24

Wednesday 25

Thursday 26

Friday 27

Saturday 28

Sunday 29

Shopping:

- [ ]
- [ ]
- [ ]
- [ ]
- [ ]
- [ ]
- [ ]
- [ ]
- [ ]
- [ ]
- [ ]
- [ ]

Notes:

June

M	T	W	T	F	S	S
						1
2	3	4	5	6	7	8
9	10	11	12	13	14	15
16	17	18	19	20	21	22
23	24	25	26	27	28	29
30						

July 2025

Monday 30

Tuesday 1

Wednesday 2

Thursday 3

Friday 4
Independence Day

Saturday 5

Sunday 6

Shopping:

- [ ]
- [ ]
- [ ]
- [ ]
- [ ]
- [ ]
- [ ]
- [ ]
- [ ]
- [ ]
- [ ]
- [ ]

Notes:

July

M	T	W	T	F	S	S
	1	2	3	4	5	6
7	8	9	10	11	12	13
14	15	16	17	18	19	20
21	22	23	24	25	26	27
28	29	30	31			

July 2025

Monday 7

Tuesday 8

Wednesday 9

Thursday 10

Friday 11

Saturday 12

Sunday 13

Shopping:

- [ ]
- [ ]
- [ ]
- [ ]
- [ ]
- [ ]
- [ ]
- [ ]
- [ ]
- [ ]
- [ ]
- [ ]

Notes:

July

M	T	W	T	F	S	S
	1	2	3	4	5	6
7	8	9	10	11	12	13
14	15	16	17	18	19	20
21	22	23	24	25	26	27
28	29	30	31			

July 2025

Monday 14

Tuesday 15

Wednesday 16

Thursday 17

Friday 18

Saturday 19

Sunday 20

Shopping:

- [ ]
- [ ]
- [ ]
- [ ]
- [ ]
- [ ]
- [ ]
- [ ]
- [ ]
- [ ]
- [ ]
- [ ]

Notes:

July

M	T	W	T	F	S	S
	1	2	3	4	5	6
7	8	9	10	11	12	13
14	15	16	17	18	19	20
21	22	23	24	25	26	27
28	29	30	31			

July 2025

Monday 21

Tuesday 22

Wednesday 23

Thursday 24

Friday 25

Saturday 26

Sunday 27

Shopping:

Notes:

July

M	T	W	T	F	S	S
	1	2	3	4	5	6
7	8	9	10	11	12	13
14	15	16	17	18	19	20
21	22	23	24	25	26	27
28	29	30	31			

July 2025

Monday 28

Tuesday 29

Wednesday 30

Thursday 31

Friday 1

Saturday 2

Sunday 3

Shopping:

Notes:

July

M	T	W	T	F	S	S
	1	2	3	4	5	6
7	8	9	10	11	12	13
14	15	16	17	18	19	20
21	22	23	24	25	26	27
28	29	30	31			

August 2025

Monday 4

Tuesday 5

Wednesday 6

Thursday 7

Friday 8

Saturday 9

Sunday 10

Shopping:

Notes:

August

M	T	W	T	F	S	S
				1	2	3
4	5	6	7	8	9	10
11	12	13	14	15	16	17
18	19	20	21	22	23	24
25	26	27	28	29	30	31

August 2025

Monday 11

Tuesday 12

Wednesday 13

Thursday 14

Friday 15

Saturday 16

Sunday 17

Shopping:

Notes:

August

M	T	W	T	F	S	S
				1	2	3
4	5	6	7	8	9	10
11	12	13	14	15	16	17
18	19	20	21	22	23	24
25	26	27	28	29	30	31

August 2025

Monday 18

Tuesday 19

Wednesday 20

Thursday 21

Friday 22

Saturday 23

Sunday 24

Shopping:

- [ ]
- [ ]
- [ ]
- [ ]
- [ ]
- [ ]
- [ ]
- [ ]
- [ ]
- [ ]
- [ ]
- [ ]

Notes:

August

M	T	W	T	F	S	S
				1	2	3
4	5	6	7	8	9	10
11	12	13	14	15	16	17
18	19	20	21	22	23	24
25	26	27	28	29	30	31

August 2025

Monday 25

Tuesday 26

Wednesday 27

Thursday 28

Friday 29

Saturday 30

Sunday 31

Shopping:

- [ ]
- [ ]
- [ ]
- [ ]
- [ ]
- [ ]
- [ ]
- [ ]
- [ ]
- [ ]
- [ ]
- [ ]

Notes:

August

M	T	W	T	F	S	S
				1	2	3
4	5	6	7	8	9	10
11	12	13	14	15	16	17
18	19	20	21	22	23	24
25	26	27	28	29	30	31

September 2025

Monday 1

Labor Day

Tuesday 2

Wednesday 3

Thursday 4

Friday 5

Saturday 6

Sunday 7

Shopping:

- [ ]
- [ ]
- [ ]
- [ ]
- [ ]
- [ ]
- [ ]
- [ ]
- [ ]
- [ ]
- [ ]
- [ ]

Notes:

September

M	T	W	T	F	S	S
1	2	3	4	5	6	7
8	9	10	11	12	13	14
15	16	17	18	19	20	21
22	23	24	25	26	27	28
29	30					

September 2025

Monday 8

Tuesday 9

Wednesday 10

Thursday 11

Friday 12

Saturday 13

Sunday 14

Shopping:

Notes:

September

M	T	W	T	F	S	S
1	2	3	4	5	6	7
8	9	10	11	12	13	14
15	16	17	18	19	20	21
22	23	24	25	26	27	28
29	30					

September 2025

Monday 15

Tuesday 16

Wednesday 17

Thursday 18

Friday 19

Saturday 20

Sunday 21

Shopping:

- [ ]
- [ ]
- [ ]
- [ ]
- [ ]
- [ ]
- [ ]
- [ ]
- [ ]
- [ ]
- [ ]
- [ ]

Notes:

September

M	T	W	T	F	S	S
1	2	3	4	5	6	7
8	9	10	11	12	13	14
15	16	17	18	19	20	21
22	23	24	25	26	27	28
29	30					

September 2025

Monday 22

Welcome to Fall

Tuesday 23

Wednesday 24

Thursday 25

Friday 26

Saturday 27

Sunday 28

Shopping:

- [ ]
- [ ]
- [ ]
- [ ]
- [ ]
- [ ]
- [ ]
- [ ]
- [ ]
- [ ]
- [ ]
- [ ]

Notes:

September

M	T	W	T	F	S	S
1	2	3	4	5	6	7
8	9	10	11	12	13	14
15	16	17	18	19	20	21
22	23	24	25	26	27	28
29	30					

October 2025

Monday 29

Tuesday 30

Wednesday 1

Thursday 2

Friday 3

Saturday 4

Sunday 5

Shopping:

- [ ]
- [ ]
- [ ]
- [ ]
- [ ]
- [ ]
- [ ]
- [ ]
- [ ]
- [ ]
- [ ]
- [ ]

Notes:

October

M	T	W	T	F	S	S
		1	2	3	4	5
6	7	8	9	10	11	12
13	14	15	16	17	18	19
20	21	22	23	24	25	26
27	28	29	30	31		

October 2025

Monday 6

Tuesday 7

Wednesday 8

Thursday 9

Friday 10

Saturday 11

Sunday 12

Shopping:

Notes:

October

M	T	W	T	F	S	S
		1	2	3	4	5
6	7	8	9	10	11	12
13	14	15	16	17	18	19
20	21	22	23	24	25	26
27	28	29	30	31		

October 2025

Monday 13
Columbus Day

Tuesday 14

Wednesday 15

Thursday 16

Friday 17

Saturday 18

Sunday 19

Shopping:

Notes:

October

M	T	W	T	F	S	S
		1	2	3	4	5
6	7	8	9	10	11	12
13	14	15	16	17	18	19
20	21	22	23	24	25	26
27	28	29	30	31		

October 2025

Monday 20

Tuesday 21

Wednesday 22

Thursday 23

Friday 24

Saturday 25

Sunday 26

Shopping:

- [ ]
- [ ]
- [ ]
- [ ]
- [ ]
- [ ]
- [ ]
- [ ]
- [ ]
- [ ]
- [ ]
- [ ]

Notes:

October

M	T	W	T	F	S	S
		1	2	3	4	5
6	7	8	9	10	11	12
13	14	15	16	17	18	19
20	21	22	23	24	25	26
27	28	29	30	31		

October 2025

Monday 27

Tuesday 28

Wednesday 29

Thursday 30

Friday 31

Halloween

Saturday 1

Sunday 2

Shopping:

- [ ]
- [ ]
- [ ]
- [ ]
- [ ]
- [ ]
- [ ]
- [ ]
- [ ]
- [ ]
- [ ]
- [ ]

Notes:

October

M	T	W	T	F	S	S
		1	2	3	4	5
6	7	8	9	10	11	12
13	14	15	16	17	18	19
20	21	22	23	24	25	26
27	28	29	30	31		

November 2025

Monday 3

Tuesday 4

Wednesday 5

Thursday 6

Friday 7

Saturday 8

Sunday 9

Shopping:

Notes:

November

M	T	W	T	F	S	S
					1	2
3	4	5	6	7	8	9
10	11	12	13	14	15	16
17	18	19	20	21	22	23
24	25	26	27	28	29	30

November 2025

Monday 10

Tuesday 11
Veterans Day

Wednesday 12

Thursday 13

Friday 14

Saturday 15

Sunday 16

Shopping:

- [ ]
- [ ]
- [ ]
- [ ]
- [ ]
- [ ]
- [ ]
- [ ]
- [ ]
- [ ]
- [ ]
- [ ]

Notes:

November

M	T	W	T	F	S	S
					1	2
3	4	5	6	7	8	9
10	11	12	13	14	15	16
17	18	19	20	21	22	23
24	25	26	27	28	29	30

November 2025

Monday 17

Tuesday 18

Wednesday 19

Thursday 20

Friday 21

Saturday 22

Sunday 23

Shopping:

Notes:

November

M	T	W	T	F	S	S
					1	2
3	4	5	6	7	8	9
10	11	12	13	14	15	16
17	18	19	20	21	22	23
24	25	26	27	28	29	30

November 2025

Monday 24

Tuesday 25

Wednesday 26

Thursday 27

Thanksgiving Day

Friday 28

Saturday 29

Sunday 30

Shopping:

- [ ]
- [ ]
- [ ]
- [ ]
- [ ]
- [ ]
- [ ]
- [ ]
- [ ]
- [ ]
- [ ]
- [ ]

Notes:

November

M	T	W	T	F	S	S
					1	2
3	4	5	6	7	8	9
10	11	12	13	14	15	16
17	18	19	20	21	22	23
24	25	26	27	28	29	30

December 2025

Monday 1

Tuesday 2

Wednesday 3

Thursday 4

Friday 5

Saturday 6

Sunday 7

Shopping:

- [ ]
- [ ]
- [ ]
- [ ]
- [ ]
- [ ]
- [ ]
- [ ]
- [ ]
- [ ]
- [ ]
- [ ]

Notes:

December

M	T	W	T	F	S	S
1	2	3	4	5	6	7
8	9	10	11	12	13	14
15	16	17	18	19	20	21
22	23	24	25	26	27	28
29	30	31				

December 2025

Monday 8

Tuesday 9

Wednesday 10

Thursday 11

Friday 12

Saturday 13

Sunday 14

Shopping:

Notes:

December

M	T	W	T	F	S	S
1	2	3	4	5	6	7
8	9	10	11	12	13	14
15	16	17	18	19	20	21
22	23	24	25	26	27	28
29	30	31				

December 2025

Monday 15

Tuesday 16

Wednesday 17

Thursday 18

Friday 19

Saturday 20

Sunday 21

Shopping:

- [ ]
- [ ]
- [ ]
- [ ]
- [ ]
- [ ]
- [ ]
- [ ]
- [ ]
- [ ]
- [ ]
- [ ]

Notes:

December

M	T	W	T	F	S	S
1	2	3	4	5	6	7
8	9	10	11	12	13	14
15	16	17	18	19	20	21
22	23	24	25	26	27	28
29	30	31				

December 2025

Monday 22

Tuesday 23

Wednesday 24
Christmas Eve

Thursday 25
Christmas Day

Friday 26

Saturday 27

Sunday 28

Shopping:

- [ ]
- [ ]
- [ ]
- [ ]
- [ ]
- [ ]
- [ ]
- [ ]
- [ ]
- [ ]
- [ ]
- [ ]

Notes:

December

M	T	W	T	F	S	S
1	2	3	4	5	6	7
8	9	10	11	12	13	14
15	16	17	18	19	20	21
22	23	24	25	26	27	28
29	30	31				

January 2026

Monday 29

Tuesday 30

Wednesday 31

New Year's Eve

Thursday 1

New Year's Day

Friday 2

Saturday 3

Sunday 4

Shopping:

Notes:

January

M	T	W	T	F	S	S
			1	2	3	4
5	6	7	8	9	10	11
12	13	14	15	16	17	18
19	20	21	22	23	24	25
26	27	28	29	30	31	

January 2026

Monday 5

Tuesday 6

Wednesday 7

Thursday 8

Friday 9

Saturday 10

Sunday 11

Shopping:

- [ ]
- [ ]
- [ ]
- [ ]
- [ ]
- [ ]
- [ ]
- [ ]
- [ ]
- [ ]
- [ ]
- [ ]

Notes:

January

M	T	W	T	F	S	S
			1	2	3	4
5	6	7	8	9	10	11
12	13	14	15	16	17	18
19	20	21	22	23	24	25
26	27	28	29	30	31	

January 2026

Monday 12

Tuesday 13

Wednesday 14

Thursday 15

Friday 16

Saturday 17

Sunday 18

Shopping:

Notes:

January

M	T	W	T	F	S	S
			1	2	3	4
5	6	7	8	9	10	11
12	13	14	15	16	17	18
19	20	21	22	23	24	25
26	27	28	29	30	31	

January 2026

Monday 19
Martin Luther King Jr. Day

Tuesday 20

Wednesday 21

Thursday 22

Friday 23

Saturday 24

Sunday 25

Shopping:

- [ ]
- [ ]
- [ ]
- [ ]
- [ ]
- [ ]
- [ ]
- [ ]
- [ ]
- [ ]
- [ ]
- [ ]

Notes:

January

M	T	W	T	F	S	S
			1	2	3	4
5	6	7	8	9	10	11
12	13	14	15	16	17	18
19	20	21	22	23	24	25
26	27	28	29	30	31	

January 2026

Monday 26

Tuesday 27

Wednesday 28

Thursday 29

Friday 30

Saturday 31

Sunday 1

Shopping:

Notes:

January

M	T	W	T	F	S	S
			1	2	3	4
5	6	7	8	9	10	11
12	13	14	15	16	17	18
19	20	21	22	23	24	25
26	27	28	29	30	31	

February 2026

Monday 2

Tuesday 3

Wednesday 4

Thursday 5

Friday 6

Saturday 7

Sunday 8

Shopping:

- [ ]
- [ ]
- [ ]
- [ ]
- [ ]
- [ ]
- [ ]
- [ ]
- [ ]
- [ ]
- [ ]
- [ ]

Notes:

February

M	T	W	T	F	S	S
						1
2	3	4	5	6	7	8
9	10	11	12	13	14	15
16	17	18	19	20	21	22
23	24	25	26	27	28	

February 2026

Monday 9

Tuesday 10

Wednesday 11

Thursday 12

Friday 13

Saturday 14

Valentine's Day

Sunday 15

Shopping:

- [ ]
- [ ]
- [ ]
- [ ]
- [ ]
- [ ]
- [ ]
- [ ]
- [ ]
- [ ]
- [ ]
- [ ]

Notes:

February

M	T	W	T	F	S	S
						1
2	3	4	5	6	7	8
9	10	11	12	13	14	15
16	17	18	19	20	21	22
23	24	25	26	27	28	

February 2026

Monday 16
Washington's Birthday

Tuesday 17

Wednesday 18

Thursday 19

Friday 20

Saturday 21

Sunday 22

Shopping:

Notes:

February

M	T	W	T	F	S	S
						1
2	3	4	5	6	7	8
9	10	11	12	13	14	15
16	17	18	19	20	21	22
23	24	25	26	27	28	

February 2026

Monday 23

Tuesday 24

Wednesday 25

Thursday 26

Friday 27

Saturday 28

Sunday 1

Shopping:

- [ ]
- [ ]
- [ ]
- [ ]
- [ ]
- [ ]
- [ ]
- [ ]
- [ ]
- [ ]
- [ ]
- [ ]

Notes:

February

M	T	W	T	F	S	S
						1
2	3	4	5	6	7	8
9	10	11	12	13	14	15
16	17	18	19	20	21	22
23	24	25	26	27	28	

March 2026

Monday 2

Tuesday 3

Wednesday 4

Thursday 5

Friday 6

Saturday 7

Sunday 8

Shopping:

- [ ]
- [ ]
- [ ]
- [ ]
- [ ]
- [ ]
- [ ]
- [ ]
- [ ]
- [ ]
- [ ]
- [ ]

Notes:

March

M	T	W	T	F	S	S
						1
2	3	4	5	6	7	8
9	10	11	12	13	14	15
16	17	18	19	20	21	22
23	24	25	26	27	28	29
30	31					

March 2026

Monday 9

Tuesday 10

Wednesday 11

Thursday 12

Friday 13

Saturday 14

Sunday 15

Shopping:

- [ ]
- [ ]
- [ ]
- [ ]
- [ ]
- [ ]
- [ ]
- [ ]
- [ ]
- [ ]
- [ ]
- [ ]

Notes:

March

M	T	W	T	F	S	S
						1
2	3	4	5	6	7	8
9	10	11	12	13	14	15
16	17	18	19	20	21	22
23	24	25	26	27	28	29
30	31					

March 2026

Monday 16

Tuesday 17

St. Patrick's Day

Wednesday 18

Thursday 19

Friday 20

Spring has Sprung

Saturday 21

Sunday 22

Shopping:

- [ ]
- [ ]
- [ ]
- [ ]
- [ ]
- [ ]
- [ ]
- [ ]
- [ ]
- [ ]
- [ ]
- [ ]

Notes:

March

M	T	W	T	F	S	S
						1
2	3	4	5	6	7	8
9	10	11	12	13	14	15
16	17	18	19	20	21	22
23	24	25	26	27	28	29
30	31					

March 2026

Monday 23

Tuesday 24

Wednesday 25

Thursday 26

Friday 27

Saturday 28

Sunday 29

Shopping:

- [ ]
- [ ]
- [ ]
- [ ]
- [ ]
- [ ]
- [ ]
- [ ]
- [ ]
- [ ]
- [ ]
- [ ]

Notes:

March

M	T	W	T	F	S	S
						1
2	3	4	5	6	7	8
9	10	11	12	13	14	15
16	17	18	19	20	21	22
23	24	25	26	27	28	29
30	31					

April 2026

Monday 30
Tuesday 31
Wednesday 1
Thursday 2
Friday 3
Saturday 4
Sunday 5 Easter Sunday

Shopping:

- [ ]
- [ ]
- [ ]
- [ ]
- [ ]
- [ ]
- [ ]
- [ ]
- [ ]
- [ ]
- [ ]
- [ ]

Notes:

April

M	T	W	T	F	S	S
		1	2	3	4	5
6	7	8	9	10	11	12
13	14	15	16	17	18	19
20	21	22	23	24	25	26
27	28	29	30			

April 2026

Monday 6
Tuesday 7
Wednesday 8
Thursday 9
Friday 10
Saturday 11
Sunday 12

Shopping:

- [ ]
- [ ]
- [ ]
- [ ]
- [ ]
- [ ]
- [ ]
- [ ]
- [ ]
- [ ]
- [ ]
- [ ]

Notes:

April

M	T	W	T	F	S	S
		1	2	3	4	5
6	7	8	9	10	11	12
13	14	15	16	17	18	19
20	21	22	23	24	25	26
27	28	29	30			

April 2026

Monday 13

Tuesday 14

Wednesday 15

Tax Day

Thursday 16

Friday 17

Saturday 18

Sunday 19

Shopping:

- [ ]
- [ ]
- [ ]
- [ ]
- [ ]
- [ ]
- [ ]
- [ ]
- [ ]
- [ ]
- [ ]
- [ ]

Notes:

April

M	T	W	T	F	S	S
		1	2	3	4	5
6	7	8	9	10	11	12
13	14	15	16	17	18	19
20	21	22	23	24	25	26
27	28	29	30			

April 2026

Monday 20

Tuesday 21

Wednesday 22

Thursday 23

Friday 24

Saturday 25

Sunday 26

Shopping:

- [ ]
- [ ]
- [ ]
- [ ]
- [ ]
- [ ]
- [ ]
- [ ]
- [ ]
- [ ]
- [ ]
- [ ]

Notes:

April

M	T	W	T	F	S	S
		1	2	3	4	5
6	7	8	9	10	11	12
13	14	15	16	17	18	19
20	21	22	23	24	25	26
27	28	29	30			

April 2026

Monday 27
Tuesday 28
Wednesday 29
Thursday 30
Friday 1
Saturday 2
Sunday 3

Shopping:

- [ ]
- [ ]
- [ ]
- [ ]
- [ ]
- [ ]
- [ ]
- [ ]
- [ ]
- [ ]
- [ ]
- [ ]

Notes:

April

M	T	W	T	F	S	S
		1	2	3	4	5
6	7	8	9	10	11	12
13	14	15	16	17	18	19
20	21	22	23	24	25	26
27	28	29	30			

May 2026

Monday 4

Tuesday 5

Wednesday 6

Thursday 7

Friday 8

Saturday 9

Sunday 10

Mother's Day

Shopping:

Notes:

April

M	T	W	T	F	S	S
		1	2	3	4	5
6	7	8	9	10	11	12
13	14	15	16	17	18	19
20	21	22	23	24	25	26
27	28	29	30			

May 2026

Monday 11

Tuesday 12

Wednesday 13

Thursday 14

Friday 15

Saturday 16

Sunday 17

Shopping:

Notes:

May

M	T	W	T	F	S	S
				1	2	3
4	5	6	7	8	9	10
11	12	13	14	15	16	17
18	19	20	21	22	23	24
25	26	27	28	29	30	31

May 2026

Monday 18

Tuesday 19

Wednesday 20

Thursday 21

Friday 22

Saturday 23

Sunday 24

Shopping:

- [ ]
- [ ]
- [ ]
- [ ]
- [ ]
- [ ]
- [ ]
- [ ]
- [ ]
- [ ]
- [ ]
- [ ]

Notes:

May

M	T	W	T	F	S	S
				1	2	3
4	5	6	7	8	9	10
11	12	13	14	15	16	17
18	19	20	21	22	23	24
25	26	27	28	29	30	31

May 2026

Monday 25
Memorial Day

Tuesday 26

Wednesday 27

Thursday 28

Friday 29

Saturday 30

Sunday 31

Shopping:

- [ ]
- [ ]
- [ ]
- [ ]
- [ ]
- [ ]
- [ ]
- [ ]
- [ ]
- [ ]
- [ ]
- [ ]

Notes:

May

M	T	W	T	F	S	S
				1	2	3
4	5	6	7	8	9	10
11	12	13	14	15	16	17
18	19	20	21	22	23	24
25	26	27	28	29	30	31

June 2026

Monday 1

Tuesday 2

Wednesday 3

Thursday 4

Friday 5

Saturday 6

Sunday 7

Shopping:

- [ ]
- [ ]
- [ ]
- [ ]
- [ ]
- [ ]
- [ ]
- [ ]
- [ ]
- [ ]
- [ ]
- [ ]

Notes:

June

M	T	W	T	F	S	S
1	2	3	4	5	6	7
8	9	10	11	12	13	14
15	16	17	18	19	20	21
22	23	24	25	26	27	28
29	30					

June 2026

Monday 8

Tuesday 9

Wednesday 10

Thursday 11

Friday 12

Saturday 13

Sunday 14

Shopping:

- [ ]
- [ ]
- [ ]
- [ ]
- [ ]
- [ ]
- [ ]
- [ ]
- [ ]
- [ ]
- [ ]
- [ ]

Notes:

June

M	T	W	T	F	S	S
1	2	3	4	5	6	7
8	9	10	11	12	13	14
15	16	17	18	19	20	21
22	23	24	25	26	27	28
29	30					

June 2026

Monday 15

Tuesday 16

Wednesday 17

Thursday 18

Friday 19

Juneteenth

Saturday 20

Sunday 21

Father's Day & First Day of Spring

Shopping:

- [ ] ______
- [ ] ______
- [ ] ______
- [ ] ______
- [ ] ______
- [ ] ______
- [ ] ______
- [ ] ______
- [ ] ______
- [ ] ______
- [ ] ______
- [ ] ______

Notes:

June

M	T	W	T	F	S	S
1	2	3	4	5	6	7
8	9	10	11	12	13	14
15	16	17	18	19	20	21
22	23	24	25	26	27	28
29	30					

June 2026

Monday 22

Tuesday 23

Wednesday 24

Thursday 25

Friday 26

Saturday 27

Sunday 28

Shopping:

- [ ]
- [ ]
- [ ]
- [ ]
- [ ]
- [ ]
- [ ]
- [ ]
- [ ]
- [ ]
- [ ]
- [ ]

Notes:

June

M	T	W	T	F	S	S
1	2	3	4	5	6	7
8	9	10	11	12	13	14
15	16	17	18	19	20	21
22	23	24	25	26	27	28
29	30					

July 2026

Monday 29

Tuesday 30

Wednesday 1

Thursday 2

Friday 3

Saturday 4
Independence Day

Sunday 5

Shopping:

- [ ]
- [ ]
- [ ]
- [ ]
- [ ]
- [ ]
- [ ]
- [ ]
- [ ]
- [ ]
- [ ]
- [ ]

Notes:

July

M	T	W	T	F	S	S
		1	2	3	4	5
6	7	8	9	10	11	12
13	14	15	16	17	18	19
20	21	22	23	24	25	26
27	28	29	30	31		

18
MONTHLY

CALENDARS

January 2025

Sun	Mon	Tue	Wed	Thu	Fri	Sat
			1 New Year's Day	2	3	4
5	6	7	8	9	10	11
12	13	14	15	16	17	18
19	20 Martin Luther King Jr. Day	21	22	23	24	25
26	27	28	29	30	31	
		Notes:				

February 2025

Sun	Mon	Tue	Wed	Thu	Fri	Sat
						1
2	3	4	5	6	7	8
9	10	11	12	13	14 Valentine's Day	15
16	17 Washington's Birthday	18	19	20	21	22
23	24	25	26	27	28	

Notes:

March 2025

Sun	Mon	Tue	Wed	Thu	Fri	Sat
						1
2	3	4	5	6	7	8
9	10	11	12	13	14	15
16	17	18	19	20	21	22
23	24	25	26	27	28	29
30	31	Notes:				

April 2025

Sun	Mon	Tue	Wed	Thu	Fri	Sat
		1	2	3	4	5
6	7	8	9	10	11	12
13	14	15 Tax Day	16	17	18	19
20 Easter Sunday	21	22	23	24	25	26
27	28	29	30			

Notes:

May 2025

Sun	Mon	Tue	Wed	Thu	Fri	Sat
				1	2	3
4	5	6	7	8	9	10
11 Mother's Day	12	13	14	15	16	17
18	19	20	21	22	23	24
25	26 Memorial Day	27	28	29	30	31
		Notes:				

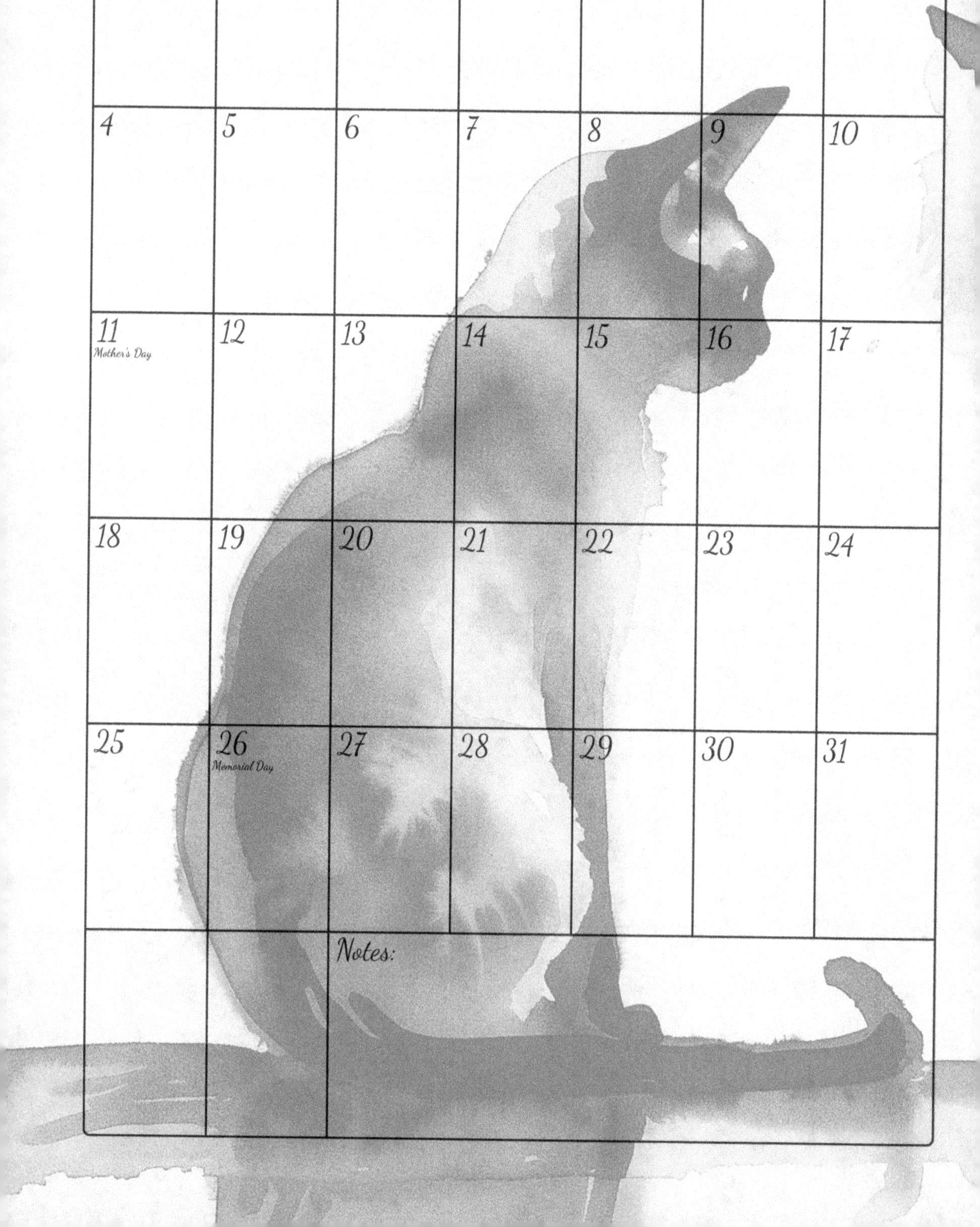

June 2025

Sun	Mon	Tue	Wed	Thu	Fri	Sat
1	2	3	4	5	6	7
8	9	10	11	12	13	14
15 Father's Day	16	17	18	19 Juneteenth	20	21
22	23	24	25	26	27	28
29	30					
		Notes:				

July 2025

Sun	Mon	Tue	Wed	Thu	Fri	Sat
		1	2	3	4 Independence Day	5
6	7	8	9	10	11	12
13	14	15	16	17	18	19
20	21	22	23	24	25	26
27	28	29	30	31		
		Notes:				

August 2025

Sun	Mon	Tue	Wed	Thu	Fri	Sat
					1	2
3	4	5	6	7	8	9
10	11	12	13	14	15	16
17	18	19	20	21	22	23
24	25	26	27	28	29	30
31		Notes:				

September 2025

Sun	Mon	Tue	Wed	Thu	Fri	Sat
	1 Labor Day	2	3	4	5	6
7	8	9	10	11	12	13
14	15	16	17	18	19	20
21	22	23	24	25	26	27
28	29	30				
		Notes:				

October 2025

Sun	Mon	Tue	Wed	Thu	Fri	Sat
			1	2	3	4
5	6	7	8	9	10	11
12	13 Columbus Day	14	15	16	17	18
19	20	21	22	23	24	25
26	27	28	29	30	31	
		Notes:				

November 2025

Sun	Mon	Tue	Wed	Thu	Fri	Sat
						1
2	3	4	5	6	7	8
9	10	11 Veterans Day	12	13	14	15
16	17	18	19	20	21	22
23	24	25	26	27 Thanksgiving Day	28	29
30		Notes:				

December 2025

Sun	Mon	Tue	Wed	Thu	Fri	Sat
	1	2	3	4	5	6
7	8	9	10	11	12	13
14	15	16	17	18	19	20
21	22	23	24 Christmas Eve	25 Christmas Day	26	27
28	29	30	31 New Year's Eve			

Notes:

January 2026

Sun	Mon	Tue	Wed	Thu	Fri	Sat
				1 New Year's Day	2	3
4	5	6	7	8	9	10
11	12	13	14	15	16	17
18	19 Martin Luther King Jr. Day	20	21	22	23	24
25	26	27	28	29	30	31

Notes:

February 2026

Sun	Mon	Tue	Wed	Thu	Fri	Sat
1	2	3	4	5	6	7
8	9	10	11	12	13	14 Valentine's Day
15	16 Washington's Birthday	17	18	19	20	21
22	23	24	25	26	27	28

Notes:

March 2026

Sun	Mon	Tue	Wed	Thu	Fri	Sat
1	2	3	4	5	6	7
8	9	10	11	12	13	14
15	16	17	18	19	20	21
22	23	24	25	26	27	28
29	30	31				
		Notes:				

April 2026

Sun	Mon	Tue	Wed	Thu	Fri	Sat
			1	2	3	4
5 Easter Sunday	6	7	8	9	10	11
12	13	14	15 Tax Day	16	17	18
19	20	21	22	23	24	25
26	27	28	29	30		

Notes:

May 2026

Sun	Mon	Tue	Wed	Thu	Fri	Sat
					1	2
3	4	5	6	7	8	9
10 Mother's Day	11	12	13	14	15	16
17	18	19	20	21	22	23
24	25 Memorial Day	26	27	28	29	30
31		Notes:				

June 2026

Sun	Mon	Tue	Wed	Thu	Fri	Sat
	1	2	3	4	5	6
7	8	9	10	11	12	13
14	15	16	17	18	19 Juneteenth	20
21 Father's Day	22	23	24	25	26	27
28	29	30				
		Notes:				

CONTACTS

Contacts

Name

Address

City State Zip

Phone

Email

Name

Address

City State Zip

Phone

Email

Name

Address

City State Zip

Phone

Email

Name

Address

City State Zip

Phone

Email

Name

Address

City State Zip

Phone

Email

Name

Address

City State Zip

Phone

Email

Name

Address

City State Zip

Phone

Email

Name

Address

City State Zip

Phone

Email

Contacts

Name

Address

City State Zip

Phone

Email

Name

Address

City State Zip

Phone

Email

Name

Address

City State Zip

Phone

Email

Name

Address

City State Zip

Phone

Email

Name

Address

City State Zip

Phone

Email

Name

Address

City State Zip

Phone

Email

Name

Address

City State Zip

Phone

Email

Name

Address

City State Zip

Phone

Email

Contacts

Name

Address

City State Zip

Phone

Email

Name

Address

City State Zip

Phone

Email

Name

Address

City State Zip

Phone

Email

Name

Address

City State Zip

Phone

Email

Name

Address

City State Zip

Phone

Email

Name

Address

City State Zip

Phone

Email

Name

Address

City State Zip

Phone

Email

Name

Address

City State Zip

Phone

Email

Contacts

Name

Address

City State Zip

Phone

Email

Name

Address

City State Zip

Phone

Email

Name

Address

City State Zip

Phone

Email

Name

Address

City State Zip

Phone

Email

Name

Address

City State Zip

Phone

Email

Name

Address

City State Zip

Phone

Email

Name

Address

City State Zip

Phone

Email

Name

Address

City State Zip

Phone

Email

Contacts

Name

Address

City State Zip

Phone

Email

Name

Address

City State Zip

Phone

Email

Name

Address

City State Zip

Phone

Email

Name

Address

City State Zip

Phone

Email

Name

Address

City State Zip

Phone

Email

Name

Address

City State Zip

Phone

Email

Name

Address

City State Zip

Phone

Email

Name

Address

City State Zip

Phone

Email

Contacts

Name

Address

City State Zip

Phone

Email

Name

Address

City State Zip

Phone

Email

Name

Address

City State Zip

Phone

Email

Name

Address

City State Zip

Phone

Email

Name

Address

City State Zip

Phone

Email

Name

Address

City State Zip

Phone

Email

Name

Address

City State Zip

Phone

Email

Name

Address

City State Zip

Phone

Email

PASSWORDS

PASSWORD TRACKER

WEBSITE:	USERNAME:
EMAIL:	PASSWORD #1:
PASSWORD #2:	PASSWORD #3:
NOTES:	

WEBSITE:	USERNAME:
EMAIL:	PASSWORD #1:
PASSWORD #2:	PASSWORD #3:
NOTES:	

WEBSITE:	USERNAME:
EMAIL:	PASSWORD #1:
PASSWORD #2:	PASSWORD #3:
NOTES:	

WEBSITE:	USERNAME:
EMAIL:	PASSWORD #1:
PASSWORD #2:	PASSWORD #3:
NOTES:	

Password Tracker

WEBSITE:	USERNAME:
EMAIL:	PASSWORD #1:
PASSWORD #2:	PASSWORD #3:
NOTES:	

WEBSITE:	USERNAME:
EMAIL:	PASSWORD #1:
PASSWORD #2:	PASSWORD #3:
NOTES:	

WEBSITE:	USERNAME:
EMAIL:	PASSWORD #1:
PASSWORD #2:	PASSWORD #3:
NOTES:	

WEBSITE:	USERNAME:
EMAIL:	PASSWORD #1:
PASSWORD #2:	PASSWORD #3:
NOTES:	

PASSWORD TRACKER

WEBSITE:	USERNAME:
EMAIL:	PASSWORD #1:
PASSWORD #2:	PASSWORD #3:
NOTES:	

WEBSITE:	USERNAME:
EMAIL:	PASSWORD #1:
PASSWORD #2:	PASSWORD #3:
NOTES:	

WEBSITE:	USERNAME:
EMAIL:	PASSWORD #1:
PASSWORD #2:	PASSWORD #3:
NOTES:	

WEBSITE:	USERNAME:
EMAIL:	PASSWORD #1:
PASSWORD #2:	PASSWORD #3:
NOTES:	

PASSWORD TRACKER

WEBSITE:	USERNAME:
EMAIL:	PASSWORD #1:
PASSWORD #2:	PASSWORD #3:
NOTES:	

WEBSITE:	USERNAME:
EMAIL:	PASSWORD #1:
PASSWORD #2:	PASSWORD #3:
NOTES:	

WEBSITE:	USERNAME:
EMAIL:	PASSWORD #1:
PASSWORD #2:	PASSWORD #3:
NOTES:	

WEBSITE:	USERNAME:
EMAIL:	PASSWORD #1:
PASSWORD #2:	PASSWORD #3:
NOTES:	

NOTES
MEOW

Meow

Meow

Meow

Meow

Meow

Meow

Meow

Meow

Meow

Meow

Love The Art of the Cat?
Please share recommendations
& honest reviews online.
Your feedback helps my small press
grow & boosts this book's visibility in
sales algorithms.
Thank you! - Nola

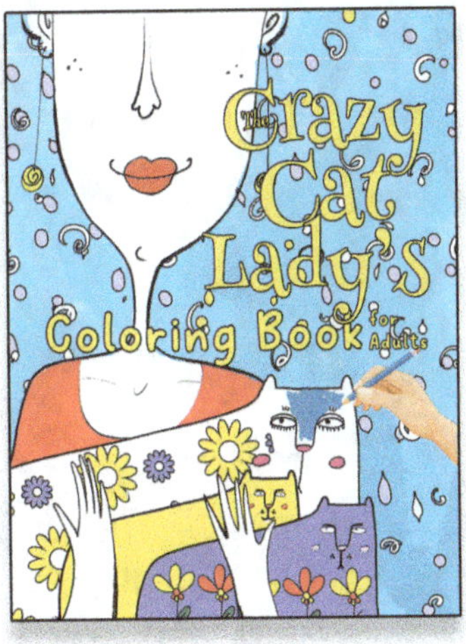

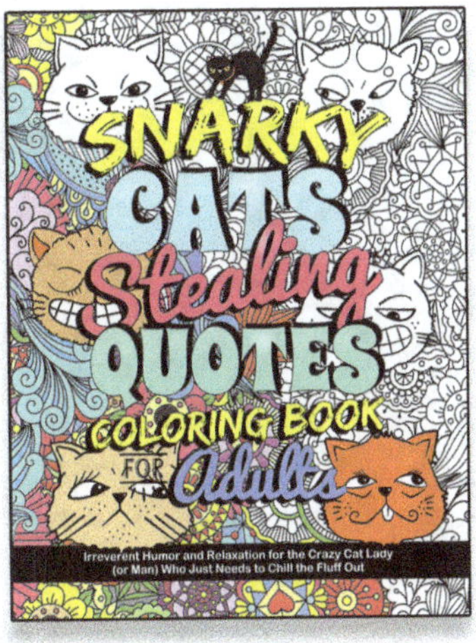

Discover these great books by
Nola Lee Kelsey
www.SoggyNomadPress.com

www.ingramcontent.com/pod-product-compliance
Lightning Source LLC
Chambersburg PA
CBHW081330120626
46546CB00011B/3279